ENDORSEMENTS

"I have known Nancy Alcorn for many years and have always admired her compassion for and dedication to young women in need. The *Mercy for . . .* series examines real problems faced by young women today and provides the answers they need to move from a life of hurt and disappointment to one of hope and freedom."

—Victoria Osteen
Co-pastor, Lakewood Church

"I know all too well how the world places an overemphasis on what we see on the outside, and girls often resort to self-destructive patterns. I personally support the work of Mercy Ministries because I have seen first hand the changed lives."

—Niki Taylor
International Supermodel

"Mercy Ministries is not afraid to deal with the ugly, tough stuff—sexual abuse, cutting, addictions, eating disorders. Nancy and her Mercy Ministries team get to the core issues. If you have a daughter, work with girls, or are a young woman struggling with these issues . . . you want to hear what Nancy has to say. It is sure to change your life."

—CeCe Winans
Grammy Award-Winning Recording Artist

"I have personally known young women who have found healing through the principles in these books. This series is very timely in an age where little hope is given for young women struggling with these issues. Nancy Alcorn is not afraid to tell the truth and offer real hope through forgiveness and restoration. If you are desperate for hope or affected by a hopeless life, read through this series and find real answers."

—Sue Semrau
Head Women's Basketball Coach, Florida State University

"As a father of two girls in their late teens, I certainly know what girls face today. I have watched Nancy Alcorn and Mercy Ministries bring hope and healing to struggling young women for many years—young women who are completely without hope. The *Mercy for . . .* series reveals the Mercy Ministries difference and offers great inspiration, hope, and a way to true healing for all who want to be free."

—Dave Ramsey
Financial Expert and Author of *The Total Money Makeover*

VIOLATED

THE **MERCY FOR** SERIES

VIOLATED

Mercy for Sexual Abuse

NANCY ALCORN

WINEPRESS **WP** PUBLISHING

WinePress Publishing (PO Box 428, Enumclaw, WA 98022) functions only as book publisher. As such, the ultimate design, content, editorial accuracy, and views expressed or implied in this work are those of the author.

This book contains advice and information relating to mental and physical health. It is not intended to replace medical advice and should be used to supplement rather than replace regular care by your physician or mental health care professional. Readers are encouraged to consult their physicians or mental health care professionals with specific questions and concerns.

Unless otherwise noted, all Scriptures are taken from the *Holy Bible, New International Version*®, *NIV*®. Copyright © 1973, 1978, 1984 by the International Bible Society. Used by permission of Zondervan. All rights reserved.

Scripture quotations marked NLT are taken from the *Holy Bible, New Living Translation*, copyright © 1996, 2004. Used by permission of Tyndale House Publishers, Inc., Wheaton, Illinois 60189. All rights reserved.

Scripture quotations marked MSG are taken from THE MESSAGE, copyright © 1993, 1994, 1995, 1996, 2000, 2001, 2002. Used by permission of NavPress Publishing Group.

Scripture quotations marked NCV are taken from the New Century Version. Copyright © 1987, 1988, 1991 by Word Publishing, a division of Thomas Nelson, Inc. Used by permission. All rights reserved.

Scripture quotations marked NKJV are taken from the New King James Version. Copyright © 1982 by Thomas Nelson, Inc. Used by permission. All rights reserved.

ISBN 13: 978-1-57921-933-8
ISBN 10: 1-57921-933-0
Library of Congress Catalog Card Number: 2007937887

DEDICATION

To those who are **desperate** for help
but feel there is no hope.
This book has been placed in your **hands** for a reason—
it is no accident that you are reading this even now.
My **prayer** is that you will read on,
because this book was written for you.
If you receive its message,
you will **never** be the same!

—*Nancy Alcorn*

CONTENTS

ACKNOWLEDGMENTS

I would like to thank the Mercy Ministries' staff members who have spent countless hours working on this manuscript with a heart to help people—Sherry Douglas, Sharon Manuel, Cissy Etheridge, Cassidy Carlgren, Amanda Phillips, and Ima Dixon.

Thanks to the Mercy residents who read the manuscript and provided honest feedback, helping to ensure the most meaningful and relevant material.

I offer a heartfelt thanks to our friends and supporters throughout the world who give so generously to bring forth changed lives.

Last but not least, I have such gratitude for our faithful staff in the various homes around the world. They give so much every day, and their love and compassion is evident. Thank you for serving alongside me in this global vision. You guys amaze me!

One hundred percent of all royalties and profits from this book will go back into the work of Mercy Ministries around the world.

INTRODUCTION

I was screaming from the depths of my soul, but nothing came out of my mouth. His hands were roaming my bare skin, as I lay helpless and scared to death. I closed my eyes so tightly they hurt, and I prayed that when I opened them, he would be gone and nothing would have ever happened.

—Kara

Kara's words are only a small part of one story shared by millions of women across the world. In fact, every two and a half minutes, someone in America is being sexually abused. Alarmingly, one out of every three women has experienced sexual abuse. Sexual abuse can happen anywhere, at any time, and to anyone—and it breaks all cultural, racial, and economic barriers. Thousands upon thousands in today's society mask their torment, living in the shame of their unspoken secret. These women are rendered helpless and hopeless by shame, manipulation, and intimidation.

Sexual abuse is a horrifying reality, but it does not have to define who you are. If you have been abused, God wants to bring healing and wholeness, so you can experience an abundant life instead of simply surviving from one day to the next.

It is *not* your fault that you were sexually abused. A life of hope, healing, and freedom can be a reality for you. In Isaiah 61:3, God promises "a crown of beauty instead of ashes, the oil of gladness instead of mourning, and a garment of praise instead of a spirit of despair."

If you have been sexually abused, facing this issue may be difficult, but it is imperative that you do. Only when you are willing to acknowledge and deal with the painful experiences will the freedom and healing you so desperately desire become a reality.

Countless young women—just like you—are looking for a way out. Many have found it, and you will read some of their stories. Since 1983 Mercy Ministries has served thousands of young women from across the country and around the world from varied cultural and economic backgrounds. Young women who come to Mercy Ministries are often facing a combination of difficult circumstances, and many of them have sought prior treatment without successful long-term results, yet they graduate from the Mercy Ministries program truly transformed. They are found attending universities, working in ministries and in corporations, on the mission field, and at home raising families. Our residents are young women who are desperate for change and desire to move beyond their difficult circumstances, yet have never been able to before. But at Mercy Ministries, they find hope.

You can find hope too. This book was written to give you a clear understanding of your struggle and to help you learn practical ways to acknowledge, identify, and find healing from sexual abuse. This book is also beneficial for those who have not personally experienced sexual abuse, but desire to reach out to the victims of this traumatic reality.

You are not alone. There is hope, there is freedom, and there is mercy for those who have experienced sexual abuse.

Chapter One

WHAT IS SEXUAL ABUSE?

God created us to be sexual beings, but only within the boundaries of marriage. God designed sex as an expression of mutual love between a husband and his wife. Sex within marriage symbolizes and celebrates the covenant, or lifetime commitment, made between a man and his wife. Satan loves to take the pure gifts of God and distort them, hoping to cause us to question the character of God. One of Satan's attempts to pervert God's character is demonstrated through sexual abuse.

Webster's defines abuse as "a corrupt practice" and "improper or excessive treatment." Sexual abuse, therefore, involves people using others for corrupt and improper sexual purposes they were never created to experience.

Sexual abuse is not a new thing. Evidence of sexual abuse is recorded even in biblical times. 2 Samuel 13 tells the story of a young woman named Tamar who was raped by her brother Amnon. Overcome with lust, Amnon plotted and schemed to get his sister into his house to overpower and rape her. Two years later Tamar's other brother, Absalom, sought revenge for his sister and murdered Amnon. One horrific sin just led to another. This story demonstrates the devastating effects that sexual abuse can bring to a person and to a family.

Molly's story, too, shows what can happen when families stray from God's plan for marriage and sexuality.

Every night I would lie in my bed and listen to my parents scream at each other. I would hear my mom tell my dad not to even think he would be sleeping in the same bed with her that night, so my dad started sleeping with me. I would feel him crawl into my bed with the smell of alcohol on his breath and pull me into his arms. He told me that he was so lucky that he had a little girl who would always love him no matter what. He would rub my back and then kiss me. Not like a daddy kisses his little girl, but like a husband kisses his wife. I never said no—I was only six and was just satisfied to have his attention. I always wanted him to notice and love me, so I wasn't going to be picky about what that looked like.

Over time the kissing and touching became more frequent, and my dad was sleeping in my bed much more than he slept with my mom. He said that he loved me and would never hurt me, so I pushed the uncomfortable feelings aside—what did I know anyway? I was only a child and he was an adult, so I assumed that everything he said was right. I also knew what happened when my dad got mad, and I never wanted to make him mad. That was why he said he loved me more than he loved my mom, because I never made him angry.

—Molly

God places authority in your life to protect you and guide you, not to hurt and abuse you. Just because an adult says something is OK doesn't necessarily mean he or she is telling the truth. God does not deal lightly with those who misuse their authority by abusing others. In Matthew 18:6 Jesus said, "But if anyone causes one of these little ones who believe in me to sin, it would be better for him to have a large millstone hung around his neck and to be drowned in the depths of the sea." God will deal with those who have hurt you. You have the right to say *no* when anyone is asking you to do wrong, even if the person is an adult.

You can experience sexual abuse at any age. Anytime you are manipulated or coerced into engaging in any type of sexual activity, that is abuse. You always have the right to refuse, even if it is with someone you are dating.

> *My boyfriend told me he loved me and that if I really loved him, I would have sex with him. I loved God, and out of obedience to Him, I wanted to wait until my boyfriend and I were married to have sex. While we were watching a movie one night, he climbed on top of me and started taking off my clothes. I was frightened by how aggressive he was and tried to fight him off. He told me that I would like it and that I needed to stop being a baby. I started to cry as I felt my virginity being taken from me. I felt like I had failed God. I had dreamed of being a virgin bride, and now I was ruined. Because he was my boyfriend, I didn't think it was as wrong as it would have been with someone I didn't know. Therefore I never told anyone what happened that night. I didn't think I had the right to say no.*
>
> —Brianna

Brianna knew God wanted her to wait until she was married to have sex, but she was forced to lose her virginity against her will. It does not matter that she was in a relationship with the person who forced her to have sex. Her body was still violated.

In order to heal from that experience, Brianna has to be honest and allow God to heal and restore her. This will involve telling someone what happened and accepting the truth that God will restore her purity, so that one day she can be the virgin bride she dreamed of being. Psalm 147:3 says, "He heals the broken-hearted and binds up their wounds." By holding on to her secret, she is only preventing God from repairing her broken heart and bringing about the life He desires for her.

Sexual abuse does not always include intercourse and those who violate others are not always adults. You may have experienced abuse from an older child, neighborhood friend, or schoolmate. Here is a story of a young girl who experienced abuse by her neighbors.

The neighborhood boys always got together to play sports in a vacant lot nearby. I was the only girl, and in order to fit in, I wanted to learn how to play too. They usually just laughed, telling me to go home to my Barbie dolls. One day I begged and begged to play along. They said I could if I showed them my underwear. Being accepted was far more important than my dignity at that point, so reluctantly I gave in. They were satisfied and let me play that day. The next time I asked to play they told me I would have to pull down my underwear and show them my private parts. I was very hesitant, but they encouraged me by agreeing to show me theirs if I showed them mine. It seemed fair, so once again I agreed. The next week when I asked to play, the boys told me I had to put my mouth on their private parts until they said to stop. I was disgusted and within a few minutes, I had to stop because I knew I was going to throw up and didn't want the boys to see me sick. I ran home and immediately threw up. After I

got out of the bathroom, I told my mom what I had done
and that I didn't want to play with them anymore.

—Jenna

Because Jenna was able to be honest with her mom about what happened with her neighbors, her mom was able to pray with her, protect her, and comfort her. You may be able to share your experience with a family member, trusted friend, pastor, or a counselor. Tell someone who can help you process your emotions and help you understand the true value you have as a child of God. By exposing the truth, you may be preventing the person who hurt you from hurting other people as well.

The first step to finding healing from a past of sexual abuse is acknowledging the abuse for exactly what it was. It may seem easier to push the horrible memories to the back of your mind or even convince yourself that what occurred in your past was normal. However, as long as you are keeping your secret in the dark, you will remain in bondage to your past.

The Effects of Abuse

When the emotions you feel are too overwhelming or you don't want to believe the truth about what is going on, a common reaction is to mentally disconnect from the experience.

Across the ceiling in my bedroom I had glow-in-the-dark
stars that hung over my bed. When he would come in at
night, I would pick a star and stare at it as I felt his hands
glide across my breasts. I would dream about flying though
a galaxy full of stars and how free it would feel to hop from
one to another. Vaguely aware of his hand going into my

underwear, I would fly around in my dream world. I never took my eyes off that star.

—Kim

When an experience is too much for your mind to fully grasp, a natural response is to separate from reality by mentally removing yourself from the situation. Many people who have been abused are able to disassociate themselves to such an extent that, for years, they may not even remember they were abused.

It may be frightening as an adult to have a smell, sound, or feeling trigger memories that have been repressed for years. If this is going on in your life, it is very important that you talk to someone. Find a Christian counselor who can help you process the emotions and feelings that are being brought up by memories of your past, or these emotions may find expression through unhealthy behaviors.

Sexual abuse is usually done in secret, but often there are signs that indicate it may have occurred. Children might display a sexual knowledge that is beyond what is normal for their age. Unexplained pain, irritation, and swelling around the genital areas are also warning signs that point to sexual abuse. Children, teens, and adults who are being or who have been abused may experience depression, sleep disturbances, nightmares, frequent urinary infections, isolation from family and friends, or withdrawal from usual activities. There is often a tendency to become either obsessive or apathetic about hygiene. Anxiety, passivity or overly "pleasing" behavior, low self-esteem, self-destructive behavior, and promiscuous activity are also common indicators of sexual abuse.

Adults experience the ramifications of sexual abuse through anger, rebellion, self-harm, fear, inappropriate sexual behavior, or difficulty developing close relationships. Many people who have been sexually abused fall into obsessive-compulsive behavior patterns such as excessive bathing, teeth brushing, or hand washing due to feeling perpetually dirty.

Many victims of sexual abuse will turn to food as a source of comfort, which often develops into an eating disorder. Anorexia, bulimia, and binge-eating disorders become an unhealthy means to express emotions or control something that is external when you feel you cannot deal with your past or control your emotional response. When the memories and emotions from the abuse remain bottled up and unresolved, feelings of fear, sadness, guilt, and confusion are often manifested through extreme and self-destructive behaviors.

However, apparent evidence or symptoms of sexual abuse do not always mean sexual abuse is the cause. Other issues may need to be identified and dealt with, and seeking guidance from a Christian counselor, pastor, or mentor is an important and proactive way to identify whether the root issue is sexual abuse. No matter what the problem, seeking help is the first step in the process of healing and restoration.

Another part of the restoration process is receiving God's healing from the hurts embedded in your heart from the trauma of being sexually abused. As we will talk about later, it is very important to be able to communicate the hurt and pain behind the emotions you're feeling. It is common to feel angry at God, but it is necessary to admit and appropriately express your anger, so the healing process can begin. As you embrace the true nature of our loving God and accept the truth that God did not abandon you or cause the abuse to happen, your emotions will begin to change. This process will be explained as you read through this book.

Why?

Why would God let this happen? Where was God when I was being abused? Why me? Why didn't anyone intervene? What if no one believes me? Why do I feel so alone?

—Paige

Perhaps your thoughts, like Paige's, are consumed by questions like these every day. Paige is not wrong for asking questions—they are a natural reaction to pain. Everything you might have been taught about who God is and His character may seem like it's being challenged when something like sexual abuse occurs.

However, when you begin to see and believe that God is compassionate, loving, and merciful, it will be easier to allow Him to bring peace to your mind. Peace comes through releasing those anxious thoughts to God. "Don't fret or worry. Instead of worrying, pray. Let petitions and praises shape your worries into prayers, letting God know your concerns. Before you know it, a sense of God's wholeness, everything coming together for good, will come and settle you down. It's wonderful what happens when Christ displaces worry at the center of your life" (Philippians 4:6–7 MSG).

God Is Good

The truth is that God did not cause those awful things to happen to you. You may have a deep anger toward God, but you need to know that He is good and perfect, and anything that is not good and perfect is not from Him (James 1:17). God presents everyone with the gift of choice and the freedom to exercise free will.

Sadly, in the instance of your experience with sexual abuse, you were hurt by someone wrongly using his or her free will. We live in a fallen world where evil is pervasive, all around us. Thankfully, you have a God who loves you enough to help you put the shattered pieces of your heart and life back together. Isaiah 61:7 says, "Instead of their shame my people will receive a double portion, and instead of disgrace they will rejoice in their inheritance; and so they will inherit a double portion in their land, and everlasting joy will be theirs."

God's heart breaks when He sees your heart breaking, and He is holding out His hand to lead you out of the prison of your pain. He will be with you and give you the courage you need to tell someone you trust what happened, ask for prayer, and allow God to heal your heart.

Let Go of a Victim Mentality

You did not choose to *become* a victim of the sexual abuse you experienced, but you do have a choice in whether you want to *remain* a victim. Focusing on the abuse and continuing to dwell on asking *why* will cause you to have a victim mentality.

Those who hold on to a victim mentality feel they are justified in their hate, bitterness, and unforgiveness. The only person you are hindering by choosing to live like this is yourself. God is a God of justice, and it is important to trust Him to be your vindicator. The righteous anger of God directed toward the person who hurt you will be far more severe than what you would be capable of if you tried to take matters into your own hands. "Therefore, this is what the LORD says: 'See, I will defend your cause and avenge you'" (Jeremiah 51:36).

Trust God to be your vindicator and move forward into what God has for your future. Jeremiah 29:11 says, "'For I know the plans I have for you,' declares the LORD, 'plans to prosper you and not to harm you, plans to give you hope and a future.'" You were created for a purpose, and your past does not have to determine your future! God is gently calling you from that dark corner where you have been hiding in shame: "Arise my darling, my beautiful one. . . . The winter is past; the rains are over and gone" (Song of Songs 2:10–11). He knows you are hurting, but as you begin to lift your head again, He will hold your hand and walk with you through the healing process. Psalm 3:3 says, "You are a shield around me, O LORD; you bestow glory on me and lift up my head."

His desire for you is to be completely whole and restored. God is not the author of your pain—Satan is. By seeing yourself as a victim, you are allowing the enemy to win. Choose to rise above the evil which Satan hopes will destroy you as you walk through this process of healing. The devil comes to steal, kill, and destroy, but Jesus comes to bring you life (John 10:10). When Jesus brings life, He makes it bigger, better, and more abundant than you could imagine.

Abuse in Unexpected Places

The church was established to be a place of safety, refuge, and security; a source of healing and comfort; and a place to encourage spiritual growth. This in itself makes the church a prime target for the enemy. The Bible warns in 1 Peter 5:8 (NLT), "Watch out for your great enemy, the devil. He prowls about like a roaring lion, looking for someone to devour." Satan despises the church and he attempts to plant seeds of lust, envy, and deceit in believers, hoping to bring division and destruction.

Attending a church is very important because there we can receive spiritual strength and develop a relationship with God within a community of other believers. However, there are people who come into the church who are struggling with their own issues. They may have a secret pornography addiction or a history of abusing or being abused themselves. Because all human beings are sinful by nature, sexual abuse has happened in churches.

However, it is important to understand that abuse in the church is not from God and has never been part of His plan. Even though sexual abuse happens inside the walls of the church, or by someone who is a part of a church, that doesn't mean that all churches are corrupt or unsafe. It only means that Satan was able to bring someone into the church who inflicted pain on another person. The enemy wants to use incidents of sexual abuse in church or among Christians to keep people away from church permanently. The truth is that there are great churches all across America. Instead of being in denial, we need to learn how to deal with these things appropriately and help people understand them.

This is a true story from a young girl named Joy:

He was an influential spiritual leader in the church my dad pastored. I was being home schooled, so I spent a lot of time back and forth at the church doing schoolwork in quiet offices away from the busy church-related business. He was close to my family. I grew up very sheltered as a child, and he seemed to be very attracted to my innocence. To me, being fourteen years old, he was safe because I felt like he was my friend, even though he was thirty-five and married.

The abuse began so gradually that I didn't even suspect I was being taken advantage of. We first began to connect by chatting online. I would confide in him because he was so caring and sensitive to how I felt about everything. I wasn't allowed to date, so I enjoyed this type of attention from a male. I trusted him because he was an adult. He started by giving me very flattering compliments and frequently stopping by the office where I did my schoolwork and massaging my shoulders and giving me very long intimate hugs.

One day we made plans to meet in another office that was farther away from the main offices. When we got there, he took off my clothes. He told me beautiful things. He said I was so delicate, fragile, and beautiful, and that he would never do anything to hurt me. I took the blame because I wasn't a baby, but a teenager, and I was letting him do this to me. I was scared that I would get in trouble if anyone ever found out. It continued little by little, and I was so confused by everything that was going on that I kept silent. We were in the office of the church. . . . as soon as he would hear someone enter the office he would throw my clothes back on me, leave me to dress, and welcome the customer with a joyous "Christian" voice and attitude.

I was full of shame, yet so fascinated by the attention that I began lying to my parents in order to be alone with him. I would tell my parents that I was going with him and his wife, but he took me places without her, pretending and treating me like I was his girlfriend. I justified the whole thing because he was an adult, so technically I wasn't dating.

I never understood why no one caught on to what was going on, so I assumed I was never going to get out of this situation. The last thing I can remember was the night he threw a party for his wife's birthday. He asked me to come over to his house beforehand to help him prepare. I lied to my parents again, telling them that other people would be there to help set up. I went over there alone. When I got there, he sexually abused me, and when he was done, he just got up and left me lying there on the couch.

I felt like that year of abuse would never end. I felt that I could not so much as breathe a thought of it to anyone because I would be in deep trouble. Some time later, he and his wife left the church.

Growing up in the church, I knew who God was and had a close relationship with Him. My parents always taught me to seek after Him when I was in need. At fifteen years old, I was too ashamed to share with anyone what had happened, so I reached out for God stronger and harder than I ever had before. I knew He saw the pain I had experienced and the shame I was dealing with. I felt so safe now that He had listened to me tell my secret, and I was not alone. It took me a few years to tell my parents what happened, but it was worth it in the end. There are no more secrets, and I have never felt as free as I do now.

—Joy

Just like Joy, you have a choice to blame God for your pain and turn your back on Him, or to trust the only One who has the ability to heal your heart and set you free from the shame of being sexually abused—no matter where it happened or who made the choice to do it.

Chapter Two

BREAKING FREE

I want to wake up from this nightmare! When I walk down the street, I look over my shoulder every few steps. I jump at the slightest touch and scream at the softest noise that catches me off guard. Paralyzed with fear, I constantly feel someone lurking behind me . . . watching me. I live haunted by abuse that ended over four years ago.

—Aly

Making a choice to break free from the bondage of your past is a huge step in the right direction. When you acknowledge what happened, you make a decision not to let it control the rest of your life. Once you make that decision, you have to go through a healing process that can be painful, but it's necessary to look at and uncover all the areas that were damaged during the trauma of sexual abuse. Find a counselor or a mature believer whom you trust to walk through this process with you.

This process involves you opening up and being vulnerable with God and others. You'll need to be totally honest about your emotions and the feelings that may come. Even though you may feel uncomfortable and embarrassed to talk about your past, honest communication is vital to receive healing that will last forever.

Choose Love

If the only expression of love you have ever experienced has been perverted through abuse, choosing love may not come easily. You may have been manipulated in your past by people who did not know what love is. For you to be able to choose love, you have to know what love really is. True love comes from God, because the Bible tells us "God is love" (1 John 4:8). God's love is not only pure, it is endless. When you realize what true and pure love is, it will be much easier to trust in a God who loves you. 1 Corinthians 13:4–7 says, "Love is patient, love is kind. It does not envy, it does not boast, it is not proud. It is not rude, it is not self-seeking, it is not easily angered, it keeps no record of wrongs. Love does not delight in evil but rejoices with the truth. It always protects, always trusts, always hopes, always perseveres."

It may be difficult to comprehend that God is both all powerful and all loving. You may ask yourself, "If God is all loving and has the power to protect me, then why didn't He?" Because God's love is perfect, He does not force people to love and obey Him. That means He will not override anyone's free will, although unfortunately, many use their freedom of choice to do evil. God sent His Son to restore to us everything that was stolen and to deliver you from the torment of memories from your past. Revelation 12:11 tells us that Satan is defeated by the blood of the Lamb and the word of our testimony. Jesus heals us from the pain of what Satan intended, and then allows us to tell others what He has done so that they, too, can experience the same restoration, freedom, and comfort (2 Corinthians 1:3–4).

When you ask Christ to be a part of your life, you are choosing love in the purest and safest form. God loves you so much, and He wants to heal your broken heart and replace your distorted perception of love with His true love. The only way He will do this, though, is if you allow Him access to your heart. Asking Jesus to be your personal Lord and Savior is the most important decision you will ever make in your life. Not only does it entitle you to eternal life in heaven, but making that decision allows you to enter into a personal relationship with Jesus Christ. Knowing Jesus personally will change your life forever. Here is an example of a prayer you can say to invite Jesus into your heart:

Prayer for Salvation

Dear Jesus, I come to you broken and ask that you take this burden that you never meant for me to carry. I give it to you right now. I need you in my life, and I thank you that you died on the cross and bore my shame so that I would not have to live in bondage to it. I ask you to come into my broken heart and heal me. I believe you are the Son of God, I believe you died on a cross for my sin and shame, and I choose to forgive so that I can receive your forgiveness in my life. This day, I choose life. I choose you. I know it won't be easy, but I trust that you will walk with me on this journey. I choose to rest in knowing that you will help me through it all. In Jesus' name, Amen.

Shatter the Silence

Every night my dad would come into my room for our own "special time" together. He sexually abused me for nine years. I have three sisters and didn't know if they had "special time" with dad, but in case they didn't, I was not going to be the

one who caused trouble. I knew my silence kept our family
together, and everyone happy.

—Katie

Katie is not the only one who has lived years with the burden of keeping sexual abuse a secret. Maybe you cannot even admit to yourself that you are being abused, and maybe you have spent years in denial. By denying the reality of the abuse, you are denying God access to your heart to bring healing and freedom. The last thing you may feel like doing is communicating what happened in your past and the feelings and emotions that go along with it. However, light dispels darkness, so it is important that you allow what is hidden in darkness to be brought into the light. When you do, freedom will become a reality.

If you are presently experiencing sexual abuse, you need to tell a mature Christian friend, relative, or counselor about what is going on in order to get out of this unhealthy situation. Know that God never intended for you to be taken advantage of, and He wants to help you get out of the situation. Please reach out for help! The Bible says, "When they were oppressed they cried out to you [God]. From heaven you heard them, and in your great compassion you gave them deliverers, who rescued them from the hand of their enemies" (Nehemiah 9:27).

Telling someone the secret that has caused you such agony is the first step, but you still need to find someone you trust who will walk with you through the healing process.

What hinders people from being able to talk about their past is most often a deep sense of shame. Shame is that feeling of humiliation or disgrace that can come from being violated. It is so harmful because it makes people feel less valuable than they truly are. Carrying the burden of shame on the inside often finds expression on the outside. Shame can manifest as self-punishment, suicidal thoughts, hiding, or isolating yourself from those who love you. Living like that is not God's will for your life! He created you for a purpose and wants you to be healed so that you can live to your full potential. Do not let the enemy steal one more day from you! Silence breeds shame, so when you break the power of silence in your life, the shame is broken as well. God promises that He will replace the shame of your past with double blessings! "Instead of their shame my people will receive a double portion, and instead of disgrace they will rejoice in their inheritance; and so they will inherit a double portion in their land, and everlasting joy will be theirs" (Isaiah 61:7).

You may fear that once you open the door to the emotions you have suppressed for so long, you will not be able to control them. Deep down, however, the need to "stay in control" is part of the issue from which sexual abuse victims have to break free. God is faithful, and He promises to heal your broken heart and to be your restorer and protector. He loves you unconditionally, and He can be trusted with your heart and your emotions. Trust that as you let go, He will catch you and carry the load that is too much for you to bear. He said, "When you pass through the waters, I will be with you; and when you pass through the rivers, they will not sweep over you. When you walk through the fire, you will not be burned; the flames will not set you ablaze" (Isaiah 43:2).

You may not know how to talk about what happened, or you may only remember bits and pieces. Let yourself cry and trust that God can handle your emotions. You can also pray that God will gently bring back the memories to your mind so He can heal them. The most important step is that you are willing to communicate using whatever healthy ways you know.

Emotions will always find a way to express themselves, but choose a healthy expression for your feelings before they lead you down the road to a life-consuming addiction. A few ways that you can express how you feel are through talking to someone, journaling, painting, writing songs or poetry, drawing, or by making a collage from magazine clippings of pictures that represent your emotions. Share this with a counselor or someone you can trust, so this person can help you process your feelings.

Staying silent is one way to ensure further destruction in your journey through life, so you might as well shatter the silence and expose what has kept you in such a state of fear and shame.

Let Go of the Past

When you let go of what is in your hand, God can give you what is in His. Exchanging your anger, bitterness, resentment, and heartache for His peace and healing is the best trade you will ever be offered. What happened to you was wrong, and forgiveness does not excuse your abuser's behavior. Forgiveness does not mean you agree with what happened or that you release the abuser from responsibility for his or her actions. Forgiveness means releasing the task of executing justice and allowing God to fight on your behalf. You cannot change what has already happened, and letting go through forgiveness brings peace and healing.

Forgiveness is also about what God has already modeled for humankind by sending His Son to save us. He has asked that we forgive others just as He has forgiven us. This act is necessary if we want to move beyond the pain of the past into an abundant life. Although this may be difficult, holding on to unforgiveness is not hindering anyone but you. A common misconception about forgiveness is that once the offense is released, all the pain will automatically leave your heart. This is not true. Forgiveness is not an emotion or a feeling, but rather a decision. The decision to forgive is a choice made through your will that serves as the "doorway" to healing. Once you make the choice to forgive, your emotions will begin to change.

If feelings of anger and bitterness continue to linger even though you have forgiven someone, just continue saying, "I have forgiven that person, and I refuse to allow these feelings to rule my life and my attitude." When you do this, these feelings will lose their power as you allow the Holy Spirit to put more of God's love in your heart. Romans 5:5 says, "Hope does not disappoint us, because God has poured out his love into our hearts by the Holy Spirit, whom he has given us." When you verbalize the hurt and emotions, and are honest about your feelings, you can learn to leave the pain of the abuse in His hands.

During Jesus' crucifixion, He endured severe emotional and physical abuse. His death on the cross was one of the most brutal executions in history. In the midst of His pain and agony, He cried out to God, saying, "Father, forgive them, for they don't know what they are doing" (Luke 23:34 NLT). Jesus understood that, because He was God's Son, His Father would be the ultimate judge of those who persecuted Him. He interceded for them, knowing they had no idea how severely God deals with those who harm His children. God is your vindicator, and your abuser will not go unpunished. God says that when you forgive, you are allowing Him to heal your heart as you release the situation to Him. This frees you to go on with your life and not be bound by trying to take matters into your own hands.

Forgiveness empowers you to go forward. As you continually give the abuse and the abuser to God, you are being set free to live without the weight of shame, guilt, and all the tormenting emotions. Let go of the burden you are holding on to and rise above those circumstances by choosing to forgive and beginning to live the life God wants you to have. You are an overcomer and you can be free. Here is a prayer that you can say to forgive those who have hurt you.

Prayer of Forgiveness

In the name of Jesus, I choose to forgive _____ for abusing me. I thank you that I do not have to carry the burden of revenge myself, but that you have promised you will be my avenger. I understand that by forgiving those who have sinned against me, I am opening the door to your forgiveness and healing in my own life. I also ask that you work in my abuser's life so that person can experience your conviction, can repent, and be willing to change. I leave it in your hands. I thank you, Father, that I am free from this bondage. In Jesus' name, Amen.

Receive God's Healing

Allowing God to heal your broken heart is especially crucial and often the most painful part of the process. To receive healing, you must be vulnerable with God, as well as with the person who is walking this journey with you. It is also important to honestly acknowledge to yourself that you have been abused. You must accept that you have been violated and betrayed, and face the emotions you are experiencing. This also means allowing yourself to actually feel the pain and grief of your past instead of repressing it.

You are allowed to cry, and there is a release in letting the tears come. You are allowed to hurt and to be angry! It is completely normal to feel all of these things, but be careful not to stay caught in them. The purpose of feeling your emotions and pain is to help you acknowledge the truth of what you went through, and allow Jesus to heal your heart. By holding on to your own pain you are denying Him the opportunity to comfort you and take that heavy burden from you. Jesus says, "Come to me, all you who are weary and burdened, and I will give you rest" (Matthew 11:28).

Vulnerability may seem risky, but with God, there is safety. "He will cover you with his feathers, and under his wings you can hide. His truth will be your shield and protection" (Psalm 91:4 NCV). You can relax in knowing that God is trustworthy. He will never hurt you. He wants to heal the wounds that have kept you bound in shame and fear. Here is an analogy that may help you relate to this part of the healing process.

Imagine a small child who finds herself with a splinter in her foot. Knowing that admitting her injury means Dad will pull out the tweezers and pry into the wound to retrieve it brings such fear to the child that she tells no one and assumes the problem will eventually take care of itself. Over the next few days, she notices the small area around the splinter has turned into a large, swollen, painful infection. Still ruled by her fear, she refuses to show the problem area to her dad. By the next week, she is in so much pain that she can barely walk. Her father notices her limping and asks if she is OK. The child mutters a yes and hides in her room to avoid further questioning. After realizing she is in more pain than she can bear and no longer able to walk or enjoy her normal activities, she cries out to her dad and shows him her wound. Filled with compassion, the father picks up his daughter, carries her in his arms, and places her on the kitchen counter. Telling her it will hurt only for a moment, he reopens the wound to find the source—a tiny splinter of wood. Through this painful extraction the little girl cries, but it is soon over and the splinter is gone. Her foot takes a few days to heal, but with the source of the infection removed, she is restored just as good as new!

This is exactly what God wants to do in your life. The wounds from your past may have grown to be infected, affecting other areas of your life and holding you back from being who God created you to be. Even though it may seem unbearable at the moment, you need to allow God to touch that wound, find the source, and bring healing to it.

Satan wants to torment you with constant memories of the abuse, but God wants to deliver you from this mental battle. As you trust God and look to Him, He will help you identify any emotions involved with that memory. Were you scared? Did you feel betrayed? Were there feelings of shame or guilt that followed? As you are honest with God about all of these, He will come in and heal your heart, giving you truth to replace the lies that were planted in your mind so many years ago—lies like "This is my fault," or "I must have done something to deserve this," or "I must be bad or this would not have happened to me." Even though you experienced abuse, the truth is that God will restore all that has been stolen. Romans 8:37 says that "in all these things we are more than conquerors through him who loved us." You no longer have to live as a victim, because you are more than a conqueror, free from the bondage of your past. Here is a prayer you can pray as you invite God in to heal your heart:

Prayer for Healing

Lord, you are the only one who knows what is in the depths of my heart. You know the deepest secrets in my soul and the hurts and wounds of my life. I ask you to look into my heart now and bring to the surface what you want to heal. Lord, gently bring to my mind the memories you want to heal so that I can let go of the pain of my past. I ask you to come into my life and restore my heart, heal the wounds of my soul, and make me whole. Be my strength, and bring the peace only you can give. Cover me with your love and mercy. In Jesus' name, Amen!

Break the Ties

Even though I hated him, I always felt drawn toward him and didn't know why. I didn't realize then that my soul had been violated along with my body. Once I prayed and broke that tie, I felt so free and unattached from my abuser. God really is putting me back together again in my mind, body, and soul.

—Joan

A soul tie is the knitting together of two souls. This tie can bring either tremendous blessing in a healthy, Godly relationship or tremendous destruction when made outside of marriage. God created the sexual union of a husband and wife to knit their souls together, to make the two become one as they establish the covenant of marriage. In the case of sexual abuse, your soul has been violated, along with your body, and mysteriously knit with the soul of your abuser. This unhealthy connection affects the way you think and feel and the decisions you make. You may have experienced guilt for feeling attached or connected to your abuser, or you may have frequent thoughts about him or her or notice strong feelings toward that person. Those are all natural responses to an ungodly soul tie. As part of your healing, God wants to set you free from that perverse tie and restore your mind, body, and soul. Through prayer, you can break the soul tie with your abuser. Here is a prayer you can say to break the ungodly soul ties you might have:

Prayer to Break Ungodly Soul Ties

I choose to break all ungodly soul ties with _____, in Jesus' name! I thank you, Lord, for restoring me completely—physically, mentally, spiritually, and emotionally. Thank you that I can have my own identity in you and apart from anyone else. My soul is now free of ungodly ties and connections and is fully committed to you. I thank you for purifying me and helping me choose healthy relationships in my life. I thank you for cleansing me from all ungodly soul ties. In Jesus' name, Amen.

Renew Your Mind

My abuser said my purpose was to please him and that was all I would ever be good for. I believed him. He told me that no one else would ever want me because I was dirty and used. I accepted everything he told me as truth because that was all I ever knew. Once I realized the truth about who I am in Christ, I was so excited and relieved to know I didn't have to live with my head hung in shame!

—Samantha

Your past does not define who you are. The Word of God defines your identity in truth and love. God is your Creator. Therefore, He knows who you are and wants to see you living to your full potential. He does not see you based on your past, but as the precious daughter He so lovingly created. The key to freedom from your past is to align your perception of yourself with God's perception of you. You may have been abused for so long that the abuse and the shame you felt has become your identity. Do not be afraid to release the pain for fear of not knowing who you are without it. As you read God's Word, you will find who you really are in Him. He will help you create a new identity, based on the way He sees you, according to the truth of His Word. Let me explain.

A practical way to replace the lies you believe, with truth, is to first identify the lies that abuse has led you to believe about yourself. You may not even know what some of them are, but ask God to show you the lies that need to be replaced. Once you have identified some of them, write them down and begin to find out the truth by searching in the Bible. The Bible is the Word of God and the foundation for truth. As you read the Bible, God will reveal truth to you that will replace the distorted perception you have had of yourself, others, and God. Here are two examples, and there are more in the appendix of this book:

Ungodly Belief: God abandoned me when I needed Him the most.

Godly Belief: God is always with me. He is my strength and my source of hope.

Related Scriptures: "God is our refuge and strength, an ever-present help in trouble" (Psalm 46:1).

"I will fear no evil, for you are with me; your rod and your staff, they comfort me" (Psalm 23:4).

Ungodly Belief: No one, not even God, could ever love me after what I have been through.

Godly Belief: God loves me always, and nothing can separate me from His unfailing love. I choose to repent and turn to God.

Related Scriptures: "I have loved you with an everlasting love; I have drawn you with loving-kindness" (Jeremiah 31:3).

"For I am convinced that neither death nor life, neither angels nor demons, neither the present nor the future, nor any powers, neither height nor depth, nor anything else in all creation, will be able to separate us from the love of God that is in Christ Jesus our Lord" (Romans 8:38–39).

What you believe about yourself usually comes out in your words, actions, and attitudes. For example, if you truly believe you have no value outside of providing sexual pleasure to others, you may act that out by engaging in promiscuous activities. Once you replace that lie with the truth, you will begin to see yourself transformed from the inside out. By believing you are worthy and valuable, you will expect others to treat you as such by respecting your body, and you will begin to respect yourself. With God's help, you will begin to expect respect instead of abuse. Write out the new, Godly beliefs you find to replace those old lies, and speak them out loud. There are more examples of how to do this in the appendix.

Surrender

The word *surrender* may be a frightening word for you. It suggests releasing control, relinquishing something you possess. It can symbolize giving up, or it may even bring up a feeling of defeat. You might be reminded of a memory in which surrender meant allowing someone to take control over you in a perverted or demeaning way. When God asks you to surrender to Him, however, it is only so He can give you peace in return. When compared to the constant state of mental turmoil abuse brings, peace is sure to sound refreshing, but it may seem out of reach. Peace can replace your pain, but you must choose to surrender yourself to your heavenly Father, who completely understands your pain and fear.

Hebrews 4:15 says, "For we do not have a high priest who is unable to sympathize with our weaknesses." As mentioned before, Jesus was sent to earth to suffer one of the most horrendous deaths ever recorded in history. He had done nothing wrong, committed no crime, and knows more than anyone what it is like to be a victim. No one can understand better than Jesus what it feels like to desperately cry out to God for answers. On the cross, the Son of God cried out to His Father, "My God, my God, why have you forsaken me?" (Mark 15:34).

Sound familiar? He, too, has felt abandoned and rejected, but regardless of how He felt in that moment of agony, He surrendered control. Jesus knew His heavenly Father loved Him and that even when all He could see was pain, God the Father saw the bigger picture. Three days later Jesus was raised from the dead, conquering the scheme of the enemy, and bringing hope to all humankind.

Satan comes only to steal, kill, and destroy, but God has the final say in every situation if we turn to Him! So when God asks you to surrender the pain of your past, He understands better than anyone how difficult that may be.

Surrender goes beyond asking Jesus to be your personal Lord and Savior. Although that is vital, surrendering is a continual process of allowing God to be in control of your daily cares and worries. When you surrender like Jesus did on the cross, you are releasing the power of God to take your situation and use it to bring hope and freedom to others. Here is a prayer you can pray to surrender your past, present, and future to God:

Prayer of Surrender

Lord, instead of holding on to the overwhelming emotions of my past, I choose to give them to you so I can move forward toward the future you have for me. I ask you to give me wisdom and courage to follow through with my commitment to let you be in charge. I am not willing for my life to stay the same. Today, I make the choice to give you control so I can walk through my day in mental, physical, and emotional peace. Until I have developed this choice to the point where it becomes natural to me, please walk with me through every moment of the day. I will make the choice to allow you to be my strength. In Jesus' name, Amen!

Chapter Three

STAYING FREE

*Y*ou now know that freedom from your past is possible, and you have been given the principles to acquire that freedom. Whether you implement them into your life is ultimately your choice. God gives you the choice by saying, "Today I have given you the choice between life and death, between blessings and curses. Now I call on heaven and earth to witness the choice you make. Oh, that you would choose life, so that you and your descendants might live!" (Deuteronomy 30:19 NLT). Although He clearly expresses which choice He desires His children to make, God has left the final decision up to you.

Part of choosing to let go of your past is making daily decisions that keep the enemy from creeping back in, which includes taking bold steps to overcome the fear that has consumed your life and learning how to trust God and others. As you discover the truth about sex as God intended it to be, and grasp your true value in Christ, you will be able to stay free from the bondage of sexual abuse.

Once you have decided in your heart that you are willing to do whatever it takes to go on with your life, God will meet you where you are and guide you as you take steps in the right direction. He never promises that it will be easy, but He does promise that you will never go alone.

Overcome Fear

When someone has hurt you, it's natural to be afraid of being hurt again. As you begin to find ways to protect yourself, you can actually find yourself trapped by the walls you have built around you. Fear can manifest itself in various ways, including feelings, attitudes, and even daily routines and habits.

One person who has experienced sexual abuse may decide the best way to protect herself is to "hate" everyone around her in an attempt to keep people from getting too close. Meanwhile, another girl who has experienced the same trauma may have developed a strong tendency to "please" everyone around her. Both reactions are rooted in a fear of being hurt or rejected.

As a reaction to fear, you may recognize one of these patterns in your life, or you may have adopted some seemingly unusual behaviors like sleeping in your closet, showering in your clothes, or flashing the lights on and off in a room before you enter it. Many behaviors are a desperate attempt to control some part of your life, even if to outsiders they may appear completely irrational. To feel like you have to turn on and off a light switch a specific number of times before entering a room may seem odd, but in the mind of a girl who lost control at a young age, it's a reasonable attempt to reclaim a safe environment.

Can you identify any evidence of fear in your life? Many girls turn to food as a comfort and means for control by bingeing, restricting, or purging what they eat. Whatever the behavior or emotion may be, you need to see that the root is fear. It may be a fear of the abuse happening again, a fear of it happening to someone you love, or even the fear of your past being exposed.

A mother who grew up in an abusive home may be so over-protective of her children that she refuses to let them leave the house. While it is important to use Godly wisdom in protecting your children, fear should never be the motive. If you are ruled by fear, you are unable to trust God to take care of you and the ones you love. Living in a mind-set of self-preservation may seem like the safest way to live, but that is a lie. The truth is that you may think you are protecting yourself, but in reality you are just submitting yourself to a life of bondage to fear.

Once you identify some of the fears in your life, the next step is to be intentional about breaking them. Start by bringing them into the light by telling someone you trust what you are afraid of and how it is affecting your daily life. Sometimes just by talking about it, you can see how distorted your perception is, making it easier to change your behavior. You might also have to do some things in spite of your fear. If you have a fear of going out in public alone, the only way to overcome it is to just go out alone—to do the very thing you are afraid of doing. (Of course, we're not suggesting that you overcome your fear by riding the subway by yourself at two in the morning, or by endangering yourself in any way. However, going to a grocery store to buy milk might be an excellent first step in overcoming a fear such as this.) Talk with the person you have been able to confide in about your fear and your desire to overcome it. Ask her to hold you accountable and pray for you as you conquer this fear.

There is freedom from fear and the bondage of living every day with knots in your stomach or never being able to relax. God wants to bring peace to your mind so that you can enjoy your life and not dread each day. God's love is perfect, and He tells us that "Perfect love drives out fear" (1 John 4:18). Fear is very clearly not from God, and He wants to take the fear that has consumed your life and replace it with the peace and security of knowing He will protect you and avenge all who have hurt you. "For God has not given us a spirit of fear, but of power and of love and of a sound mind" (2 Timothy 1:7 NKJV). Although it may be difficult for you to step out in faith, you can be assured the arms of a loving God will support you, and the light of His Word will give you a solid place to put your feet.

Rebuild Trust

When trust is broken, walls are built. You have probably built walls around your heart, keeping relationships at a distance by hardening your heart toward those who try to get too close. The Bible talks a lot about community and the power of unity, making it a prime target for the devil to attack.

When God created man in the very beginning, He said that it is not good for man to be alone, so He created Eve, a helper. The same is true today. God does not want you to live your life in isolation, but to enjoy the life He has given you with other people who can encourage you in your walk with the Lord. "If one falls down, his friend can help him up. But pity the man who falls and has no one to help him up!" (Ecclesiastes 4:10).

While it is true that no human being is perfect, it is just as true that not every person in this world is out to hurt you! Once you find yourself rooted in your identity in Christ—the only one who will never hurt you or abandon you—then you can enjoy the relationships God has placed around you without the fear of being hurt. This doesn't mean you will never be hurt again, but it does mean that when you are secure in who you are, you will look at relationships in a completely different way. God places people in your life to love and encourage you as you daily grow in your knowledge of God and your identity in Him.

Everyone goes through hard times and experiences wounds of different magnitudes, but we are to encourage each other through these times. Once you have reached a place in your life that you feel you have experienced healing and freedom from your past, God may bring someone into your life who has been through the same pain and who desires the freedom she sees in you.

Authority

It is also common to experience deep issues with trusting authority if you were betrayed by an adult or someone in a position of authority over you. Here is a truth that will set you free from the fear of authority in your life: God never asks you to blindly trust people in authority over you solely based on their position of power or authority. God only asks that you trust and obey *His* ultimate authority with a submissive heart.

God is the ultimate authority, and He has placed people in your life that He has delegated authority to. If those He has delegated His ultimate authority to choose to misuse and abuse it, they will answer to God, and you have the right not to obey if they are asking you to sin. Let me say this more clearly: If anyone ever asks you to do something that is a sin, you can say no!

God places His authority in your life to cover and protect you. Yes, there are people who take advantage of their God-given position, and their actions have the potential to affect others, as you may have experienced through sexual abuse. Know that God does not take lightly those who abuse their position of authority or those who take advantage of His children. He promises to take vengeance on all who have hurt you—they will be dealt with.

Satan would love to use your past as a reason for you to believe that all authority is bad so that you live in a lifestyle of rebellion and disobedience, which only leads to more misery. Understanding that God has perfectly balanced authority and accountability should relieve you of feeling like you have to obey only when you agree. If you are walking away from Godly authority, you are walking out from under God's protection.

Discover the Truth

If you have experienced sexual abuse, the word *sex* probably has a very negative connotation for you. From the perspective of someone who has been sexually abused, it would only make sense for you to associate sex with something perverted and illicit. It is sad to see how far our society has gone from what God created sex to be. Yes, God created sex—He actually invented it! In the Garden of Eden, God created Eve from Adam's rib so they could be beautifully united into one. In today's culture, sex is used for advertising, illicit pleasure, and manipulation, among other things. In the Garden of Eden, sin entered the world when Eve ate from the forbidden tree. Once sin entered the world, everything that was once pure became distorted by the enemy.

You may commonly associate sex with words like *dirty, terrifying, perverted,* or *gross.* These are all words that apply to sexual abuse, but not sex! Those two things are completely different! Words that should be associated with sex are words like *intimate, beautiful, safe,* and *pure.* Song of Songs (Solomon) is a book in the Bible that paints a picture of what sex is supposed to look like. It was intended to be a beautiful celebration of intimacy between a man and his wife.

As we have already pointed out, every time you are involved sexually with someone, your soul becomes tied with his (or hers), and the emotional effects can be very damaging. Even if your purity was stolen from you, God can and will restore you to wholeness. Believing that sex is your only purpose and engaging in promiscuous behaviors is not the answer. Following that path causes more emotional damage to your heart, soul, and body. Numerous sexually transmitted diseases, AIDS, and an unplanned pregnancy can all result from sex outside of marriage. God doesn't set boundaries for His children because He wants to punish, but because He loves you and wants to protect you from more abuse in your life. As you wait for the spouse God has for you, He will restore your broken heart and renew your mind and body so you can one day experience the purity of sex in marriage as He intended it to be.

Know Your Value

Do you really know who you are? If you were truly able to grasp your identity in Christ, your entire life would change overnight. The following illustration has been depicted in many Hollywood movies over the years: You see a slave girl, doing chores and serving a master who has told her that slavery and oppression are her only purpose for existence. She is dressed in rags and hangs her head in shame as she reluctantly accepts that she was born to be a servant to everyone she meets. Then, one day, everything changes. A handsome prince rides up on a white stallion and delivers the life-altering news . . . This slave girl is actually the long-lost heiress to the throne and the daughter of a king! The servant who was used and abused all of her life is actually a princess! She stands in shock as she hears the news, and immediately, the master who has "owned" her for all these years laughs mockingly, daring her to actually believe the charming prince. She glances back at the life she has been living—a filthy mattress on the floor, torn clothes, and an empty stomach, then she looks ahead to see her charming prince waiting to take her to the royal palace. She hesitates no longer, and overnight, everything about this poor servant girl changes! She is given a soft bed on which to lay her head, a whole new wardrobe, and plenty to eat. Understanding her value and worth changes the way she walks, talks, and even how she treats others. She is now in a place to accept her position with a humble heart and use her newly acquired wealth to extend grace to all she meets.

You, too, are a daughter of the King. The transformation may not be about where you sleep or the clothes you wear. Inside your heart, you become a whole new person when you accept the truth that you are a daughter of God—a daughter of the One who created the universe. You can rest securely in the fact that God is your Protector. Know each day that He will provide what you need, and be assured that He will daily clothe you with His love and goodness.

When you read God's Word, you will see that it is filled with truths about who you are and promises He has made to you. Reading the promises of God for your life once is great, but to renew your mind from all the dark lies you have believed your whole life, you need to continually meditate on those promises and allow the truths to sink into your heart. This does not mean your life will be perfect, because it will take time for your emotions to line up with these truths. Be patient with yourself and remember that this is a process (Philippians 1:6)!

There will be some who will mock you, trying to make you doubt who you are, but you have to make the choice to believe what God says above anything anyone else might be telling you. He has come to rescue you from your old life of shame and restore to you all that was lost!

Chapter Four

STORIES OF MERCY

God provides comfort and healing to His children so that they can extend the same hope they received from the Lord to others who are in pain and bondage. Monique and Tara have allowed God access to their broken hearts and have experienced personally the life-changing healing that only He can bring. They, too, have experienced the horrible trauma of sexual abuse, but have made the decision to rise above their circumstances and release their pain to God. He is the only one who can turn your past pain into a testimony of His grace. As you read these stories of mercy, I pray that you will be filled with hope and be encouraged that God has a purpose and plan for you beyond your pain. "'For I know the plans I have for you,' says the LORD. 'They are plans for good and not for disaster, to give you a future and a hope'" (Jeremiah 29:11 NLT).

Monique's Story

Fear and shame ruled my life since age five, when a family friend, and others he invited, began sexually abusing me. The secrecy, threats, and violent acts paralyzed me internally with fear. The fear of letting the secret out was so intense that I was even fearful of someone seeing fear in me. I hated myself for what was happening to me and what I was participating in. I was certain that I was evil and dirty to the core and doomed to live the rest of my life that way.

At the age of twelve I became pregnant. When my abusers discovered this, they did things to me that made me lose the baby. The terror of all that happened threw me into a deep depression, intensifying my shame, self-hate, and confusion.

Around this time a good friend was finally able to persuade me to go to her youth group. Though I was skeptical, I had never felt love like I did there—that's what got me through week to week. I gave my life to Jesus during this time and began to grow in my relationship with God. But then my abusers threatened me, and I became afraid to continue going to church or seeking God.

Even though my primary abuser no longer had steady contact with me, things only got worse. I became consumed by an eating disorder, which helped distract my mind and gave me a way to punish myself. I also turned to self-mutilation for punishment. At least then I was able to see and understand a form of pain and know why it hurt, unlike the emotional torment I did not understand.

When I left for college I was excited to finally escape the abuse and was eager to start a new life, but it was then that a relationship with a pastor/counselor turned sexual. I began abusing prescription drugs and alcohol. At that point I began to freely give my body to guys so they would not have the chance to use me first. By my senior year of college, I was at the end of my rope, utterly desperate. I heard about Mercy Ministries and felt I had no other option, so I applied to the program.

During my wait to get into the program, I got involved with a church, and God began preparing me for what He was going to do in my life. To the extent I knew how, I chose to surrender all of myself to Him.

At Mercy, God began pouring His love on me. I did not understand or really know what was happening. I could only cry with no explanation. He taught me about His grace and that it did not matter what I did or did not do. He loved me for me, as His child, and showed me that I am completely right in Him because of Christ. I was still doubtful that He could heal the pain or free me from the addictions, but He continually amazed me as I sought Him. He lovingly and gently taught me how to trust, and as I began to slowly lower some of the barricades I had built, He was able to come in and heal my pain. He began teaching me about my true identity in Him and His incredible love and goodness.

As I let Him into some of my deepest hurts, He held me in His love and truly brought deep healing that seemed impossible. Christ has healed me from the pain of my entire past, and the power that pain used to have over my life cannot affect my relationship with God unless I let it. I had carried so much shame over the loss of my baby and felt responsible for her death by not protecting her. I hated God for letting it all happen. As I talked to Him about what happened and told Him how I felt, He wiped out the shame and showed me that my little girl is in heaven with God, safe from harm and happy. I will get to see her in heaven and spend eternity with her. God has done this same kind of deep healing in so many areas of my life, which has freed me to love Him more and follow Him. Even in the midst of all that, He set me free from the eating disorder, self-hatred, shame, depression, and addictions.

I no longer have the spirit of fear, but of power, love, and of a sound mind. I am daily amazed by His goodness and honestly believe that I know He can and will get me through anything I face because He is so good and so powerful. I know I am a different person, being made whole. He is restoring all Satan thought he had stolen from me. I am excited to be able to help others find this relationship with God and receive true life and healing because now I know life does not have to be like I thought. God is so good, and able to heal and restore if we allow Him to do so.

Tara's Story

I am now sixteen years old. From the time I was about four years old through age fourteen, several different people sexually abused me. While I may not bear much scarring on my body, unfortunately my heart did not mend quite so quickly.

I endured a lot of unhappy effects from being abused and made a lot of bad choices. Very early in my childhood, I was already in a deep depression and began doing things to hurt myself. I knew I deserved to be punished and was so used to the violence and pain that I began to take it out on myself. I was often exposed to pornography and then became addicted to it, which led to more struggles with lust and masturbation during my childhood. I had no idea how to relate to people normally or in a healthy way. Some of the consequences from that were a lot of rejection from my peers and unbearable loneliness.

For a time, I molested my sister, passing on what I knew. As things progressed and I got older, I was in a desperate place. I was living at several different people's houses until finally being told by child protective services I could not live with my biological family ever again because of the extent of the abuse that was occurring. Between various counselors, psychiatrists, therapists, mental hospitals, and government-run facilities, I was given a lot of diagnoses, but never any hope for anything different.

During my longest time as a patient in a psychiatric hospital, I applied to Mercy Ministries and was accepted. I was filled with fear and uncertainty, but that was nothing compared to all the fear, confusion, and issues that I'd dealt with for so long. I knew that if something didn't change soon, I was going to kill myself. I'd already tried many times, and it seemed I was just becoming more insane each day. I was about to break and I couldn't take it anymore.

Finally, I found a lot of healing, not by a set protocol of a certain number of steps, a bottle of pills, or by following some method, but by being led to Jesus Christ, my Savior. I had so many addictions and was consumed by self-mutilation, thoughts of suicide, an eating disorder, psychiatric disorders, and so much fear, depression, and confusion. At last I found someone who could take all that, and it didn't faze Him a bit. I'd been raised in churches, and I knew a lot about religion and theology, but I had no clue as to what God was really like. Now I do. God has sought after me faithfully and gently, never making demands of me and never being inappropriate with me. He has tenderly, yet firmly reached out to me in all my chaos, turmoil, and despondency, showing me He is all I'm so desperate for.

It has been a long journey, but I now know that healing from sexual abuse and all its effects is possible. God provided a safe place for me at Mercy Ministries and surrounded me with safe people (including safe *men*, which I didn't even know was possible!) and counselors who loved me. They didn't attempt to bring me healing by themselves, but showed me truth and brought me to Jesus. God promises to bind up the brokenhearted, and I found out He truly does. With the help of safe people, He's brought a lot of healing, restoring the part of me that had been destroyed, damaged, and twisted. In spending time with God, I've found so much healing. I hate to overuse that word, but Jesus cleansed away all the garbage that was covering me, and He placed His hands on the deep wounds that were so damaging to me. They had been so painful that I'd lost all feeling and had learned to pretend everything was fine. Jesus met me where I was. He was not afraid of all the rotten mess that was in and around me, but He stepped down, not afraid to get His hands dirty by touching me. Jesus surrounded me with His safety and protection, cherishing me and sheltering me from the raging storm. He's shown me that I was not the despicable creature I thought I was. I've allowed Him to peel away the masks, exposing all the sores, all the pain, all the weakness, and the need. Jesus showed me how He will give me what I need and how much He loves me.

Though I am not perfect, I know that in the arms of my God I am whole. He walks me along the path He has called me to, and I am enjoying my journey with Jesus, seeing my life and future totally differently—with hope. I don't want to die anymore. Jesus has freed me from my death obsession and from so many other addictions and disorders. He's freed me from thinking about suicide, self-hatred, shame, guilt, numbness, depression, and enabled me to see truth, to love truth, and to walk in truth. By following Him and receiving the truth, I am set free.

Chapter Five

FOR PARENTS AND OTHERS WHO CARE

Whether you're a dad, mom, family member, friend, or support person of a girl who has been sexually abused, helping her through the pain can be difficult. So many times, we see the individual dealing with the abuse struggling with shame and feeling very alone in her pain. Support in her life is crucial in facing the abuse and gaining freedom from what occurred. Through this chapter, we trust you will gain some understanding as to how to help your loved one deal with the abuse she has experienced.

Create an Environment for Healthy Expression

Most importantly, you must listen to the person who's been abused. Her voice has been silenced through the shame and guilt. Her strong need to be heard is crucial to the healing process. She needs to know that she can express herself openly without judgment or fear, and without being rejected or criticized.

Creating an environment where your daughter can open up and be honest about her experience cultivates the process of breaking the cycle of abuse. Whether the abuse is happening in the present or has happened in the past, the truth must come out in order to deal with the issue and bring about safety and prevention of future abuse. If the abuse is ignored or minimized, your daughter could withdraw and shut down completely. If you allow her voice to be heard and allow her to tell her story without judgment, skepticism, or interruption, you will create an environment for the truth to come forth and healing to begin. She wants to be heard, and she wants to be understood. By listening and extending compassion, you can help her to begin healing from the inner wounds the abuse has caused in her life.

Reassure your daughter of your love and acceptance. Let her know how proud you are of her for sharing her story and for being willing to get help. Assure her of your loyalty and faithfulness to see her through this until it is resolved. Let her know you will be by her side no matter the outcome. Tell her that you will protect her.

After you have heard her story, you will not only need to offer comfort to her, but you will need to decide your action plan to provide safety and counsel for her. Depending on the nature of the abuse, you will likely need to follow up from a legal standpoint.

If your daughter is a minor and has shared that she has been or is being abused by a family member who still lives in the house, you will need to put aside your personal feelings of what you have heard and report the alleged abuse. It can be a complicated situation if the abuse is still occurring and you are the abuser's spouse, but now is not the time to minimize or deny that it could be happening in your home. You will need to lay aside what you feel to take action to prevent future abuse. After reporting the incident(s) and ensuring your daughter's safety, you should explore your personal feelings with a professional. The goal for helping your daughter who is experiencing any abuse is to provide safety so that the healing process may begin.

If you are reporting the alleged abuse of a minor, you will need to call the local authorities, such as child protective services or the police in the county where the alleged abuse is taking place. If the abuse was happening in your home, you will need to remove yourself and your daughter from the home until the alleged abuse is investigated and the environment is safe.

As laws differ from state to state, you will need to explore your daughter's rights, as well as your own, concerning reporting and pressing charges.

Abuse in the Family

Abuse happens in immediate families, but your daughter may have experienced sexual abuse from a family member who does not live in your home. In these cases, be sure you are considerate of your daughter in planning family events, holidays, or reunions where she would encounter her abuser(s). By doing so, you will help your daughter to feel safe, protected, and understood. Parents who discount their daughter's allegations of sexual abuse, denying the issues and allowing the abuser to be around their daughter, contribute to her pain and ultimately prolong her healing process.

Denial can keep abuse cycling for generations. You must help put a stop to the abuse. You can create an environment that will help prevent abuse in your family. As a parent, you must stand in the gap in prayer for your family and your children. You have the authority to break generational curses or patterns in your family while providing safety for your daughter (Luke 10:19). God gives us a choice (Deuteronomy 30:19), and Galatians 3:13 tells us that in Christ the curse in broken.

Be a Support

Your support of your daughter is a wonderful extension and example of Christ's love. As you provide support, you are cultivating the healing process and moving it forward. Daughters need to know their parents hear them, believe them, and will fight for them. When a young woman is experiencing the pain of past or present abuse, she can feel helpless and hopeless. She can feel that she is not safe and is vulnerable to being hurt again. Your daughter will need to know you can and will help her through this hard time. Your daughter needs to know you will protect her.

Here are some ways you can provide support for your daughter:

- Listen
- Be patient
- Be understanding
- Offer comfort
- Ask your daughter what she needs
- Report alleged abuse
- Provide safety and protection
- Use encouraging words to affirm your daughter's value
- Accept your daughter
- Encourage your daughter to go to a Christian counselor or pastor
- Pray with your daughter

Support for Parents

Parents need support during this time as well. You will need to have people in your life that can assist you in processing what has happened to your daughter. However, be sensitive to your daughter's need for privacy, and choose people you are certain you can trust to keep your confidence. Support people need to be those you can trust and who will encourage Christian values. Those who encourage you to hide the truth are not the ones you need to listen to. You need support from those who provide Godly wisdom and who walk in truth. Examples of support are a family member, pastor, friend, mentor, or counselor.

If the abuse occurred inside the family, the shock, guilt, and shame will make it difficult to talk about the abuse. Know that exposing the abuse is vital to stopping it and to allowing healing to begin. If you hide what has happened, you will be enabling the abuse to continue. Do not let abuse ruin your life. Help both you and your daughter cope with the abuse so you both can move past it. Also, tell your daughter the names of the individuals from whom you will be seeking support. By doing so, you'll be demonstrating and fostering trust, loyalty, and honest communication.

Praying through the pain is imperative for connecting with God and allowing Him to bring healing to your daughter and your family. Here are some examples of prayers you can use to break any abusive patterns that have occurred in your family.

Prayer for Your Daughter

Lord, my God, I come to you on behalf of my daughter, and I pray for your healing power to come into her life. I pray that her heart would be mended and made whole. I pray for protection for my daughter. I pray that you would put a shield around her and that you would bring about justice. Be my daughter's vindicator for the hurt she has experienced. I forgive and release those who have hurt my daughter and pray that nothing would hinder the healing work you desire to do in her. Thank you, God, for redeeming the pain and restoring all that was stolen from her. In Jesus' name, Amen.

A Prayer for Parents to Break Generational Patterns

Lord God, I break every generational curse or pattern known or unknown from my family's life, my life, and the lives of my children. I thank you for authority to break the generational patterns and for the blessings that will be passed down to my children and grandchildren. No longer will abuse or any other curse have power over my family. In the name of Jesus Christ, Amen.

Appendix

CHANGING UNGODLY BELIEFS TO GODLY BELIEFS

*U*ngodly belief: I will never amount to anything because I was sexually abused.

Godly belief: I am more than a conqueror through Christ and have overcome the shame of my past. God has an amazing plan and purpose for my life, and He will give me the strength I need as I press toward it.

Related Scriptures: "Forgetting what is behind and straining toward what is ahead, I press on toward the goal to win the prize for which God has called me heavenward in Christ Jesus" (Philippians 3:13–14).

"But you belong to God, my dear children. You have already won a victory over those people, because the Spirit who lives in you is greater than the spirit who lives in the world" (1 John 4:4 NLT).

"'For I know the plans I have for you,' declares the LORD, 'plans to prosper you and not to harm you, plans to give you hope and a future'" (Jeremiah 29:11).

Ungodly Belief: I will always live in fear that someone will take advantage of me again.

Godly Belief: God is my protector and is with me wherever I go. I will be confident because God will take care of me.

Related Scriptures: "For God has not given us a spirit of fear and timidity, but of power, love, and self-discipline" (2 Timothy 1:7 NLT).

"For the LORD your God is living among you. He is a mighty savior. He will take delight in you with gladness. With his love, he will calm all your fears" (Zephaniah 3:17 NLT).

"For our present troubles are small and won't last very long. Yet they produce for us a glory that vastly outweighs them and will last forever!" (2 Corinthians 4:17 NLT).

Ungodly Belief: My abuser will never pay for what he (or she) did—I must get revenge for myself.

Godly Belief: God loves me and will bring justice. I can rest in peace and let God be my vindicator.

Related Scriptures: "And let the peace that comes from Christ rule in your hearts" (Colossians 3:15 NLT).

"And I will deal severely with all who have oppressed you. I will save the weak and helpless ones; I will bring together those who were chased away. I will give glory and fame to my former exiles, wherever they have been mocked and shamed" (Zephaniah 3:19 NLT).

"The LORD is slow to get angry, but his power is great, and he never lets the guilty go unpunished" (Nahum 1:3 NLT).

Ungodly Belief: God's purpose and plan for my life has been diverted because I was abused.

Godly Belief: I am a child of God and nothing can change that! He has great plans for my life and is faithful to continue the good work He started in me.

Related Scriptures: "Consider it pure joy, my brothers, whenever you face trials of many kinds, because you know that the testing of your faith develops perseverance. Perseverance must finish its work so that you may be mature and complete, not lacking anything" (James 1:2–4).

"'For I know the plans I have for you,' says the LORD. 'They are plans for good and not for disaster, to give you a future and a hope'" (Jeremiah 29:11 NLT).

"And I am certain that God, who began the good work within you, will continue his work until it is finally finished on the day when Christ Jesus returns" (Philippians 1:6 NLT).

Ungodly Belief: These emotions are too overwhelming, and no one cares how I feel.

Godly Belief: God cares how I feel, and He has great compassion toward me. I can rest in knowing that He will carry my burdens.

Related Scriptures: "Give all your worries and cares to God, for he cares about you" (1 Peter 5:7 NLT).

"Yet the LORD longs to be gracious to you; he rises to show you compassion. For the LORD is a God of justice" (Isaiah 30:18).

"For the LORD comforts his people and will have compassion on his afflicted ones" (Isaiah 49:13).

Ungodly Belief: I have been hurt too much and will never trust anyone again.

Godly Belief: God loves me, and I will trust Him no matter what. God will bring safe people into my life to love and encourage me in healthy ways.

Related Scriptures: "Trust in the LORD with all your heart; do not depend on your own understanding" (Proverbs 3:5 NLT).

"To love him with all your heart, with all your understanding and with all your strength, and to love your neighbor as yourself is more important than all burnt offerings and sacrifices" (Mark 12:33).

"If one falls down, his friend can help him up. But pity the man who falls and has no one to help him up!" (Ecclesiastes 4:10).

Ungodly Belief: No man will ever want me. I am "damaged goods."

Godly Belief: God has taken my shame and restored me to wholeness. I have confessed my sin to Him, and He has forgiven me and cleansed me. I am a virgin in God's eyes. I have been set free to enjoy my future!

Related Scriptures: "He has sent me to bind up the brokenhearted, to proclaim freedom for the captives and release from darkness for the prisoners, to proclaim the year of the LORD's favor and the day of vengeance of our God, to comfort all who mourn, and provide for those who grieve in Zion—to bestow on them a crown of beauty instead of ashes, the oil of gladness instead of mourning, and a garment of praise instead of a spirit of despair. They will be called oaks of righteousness, a planting of the LORD for the display of his splendor" (Isaiah 61:1–3).

"I have loved you with an everlasting love; I have drawn you with loving-kindness. I will build you up again and you will be rebuilt, O Virgin Israel. Again you will take up your tambourines and go out to dance with the joyful" (Jeremiah 31:3–4).

"Arise, my darling, my beautiful one, and come with me. See! The winter is past; the rains are over and gone" (Song of Songs 2:10–11).

Ungodly Belief: God abandoned me when I needed Him the most.

Godly Belief: God is always with me. He is my strength and source of hope.

Related Scriptures: "God is our refuge and strength, an ever-present help in trouble" (Psalm 46:1).

"I will fear no evil, for you are with me; your rod and your staff, they comfort me" (Psalm 23:4).

"Fear not, for I have redeemed you; I have summoned you by name; you are mine. When you pass through the waters, I will be with you; and when you pass through the rivers, they will not sweep over you. When you walk through the fire, you will not be burned; the flames will not set you ablaze. For I am the LORD, your God, the Holy One of Israel, your Savior" (Isaiah 43:1–3).

Ungodly Belief: No one—not even God—could ever love me after what I have been through.

Godly Belief: God loves me unconditionally, and nothing can separate me from His unfailing love.

Related Scriptures: "I have loved you with an everlasting love; I have drawn you with loving-kindness" (Jeremiah 31:3).

"For I am convinced that neither death nor life, neither angels nor demons, neither the present nor the future, nor any powers, neither height nor depth, nor anything else in all creation, will be able to separate us from the love of God that is in Christ Jesus our Lord" (Romans 8:38–39).

"O Israel, put your hope in the LORD, for with the LORD is unfailing love and with him is full redemption" (Psalm 130:7).

Ungodly Belief: I must hold myself together and not share how I feel.

Godly Belief: God wants me to be real about how I feel so He can provide comfort and healing. It is when I am healed and whole that I can comfort others who have been through the same things I have.

Related Scriptures: "Blessed are those who mourn, for they will be comforted" (Matthew 5:4).

"Praise be to the God and Father of our Lord Jesus Christ, the Father of compassion and the God of all comfort, who comforts us in all our troubles, so that we can comfort those in any trouble with the comfort we ourselves have received from God" (2 Corinthians 1:3–4).

Ungodly Belief: I should have kept the abuse a secret. Now I have made other people upset. I should have just kept quiet.

Godly Belief: God wants evil to be exposed. I do not need to be afraid, because God will protect me.

Related Scriptures: "He will bring to light what is hidden in darkness and will expose the motives of men's hearts" (1 Corinthians 4:5).

"Have nothing to do with the fruitless deeds of darkness, but rather expose them" (Ephesians 5:11).

"Though a mighty army surrounds me, my heart will not be afraid. Even if I am attacked, I will remain confident" (Psalm 27:3 NLT).

Ungodly Belief: Since I was hurt by someone who was supposed to take care of me, no authority can be trusted.

Godly Belief: I will choose to obey those in authority over me because I know God places people in authority for my protection and not to hurt or control me. I trust God will protect me as I submit with a willing heart and know that those who misuse their authority will answer to Him.

Related Scriptures: "Everyone must submit himself to the governing authorities, for there is no authority except that which God has established. The authorities that exist have been established by God" (Romans 13:1).

"Whatever you do, work at it with all your heart, as working for the Lord, not for men, since you know that you will receive an inheritance from the Lord as a reward. It is the Lord Christ you are serving. Anyone who does wrong will be repaid for his wrong, and there is no favoritism" (Colossians 3:23–25).

"Obey your earthly masters with respect and fear, and with sincerity of heart, just as you would obey Christ. Obey them not only to win their favor when their eye is on you, but like slaves of Christ, doing the will of God from your heart" (Ephesians 6:5–6).

Ungodly Belief: Sex is perverted and should never be enjoyed.

Godly Belief: Sex was God's idea. God created a man and a woman to enjoy sex within the boundaries of marriage. It is a beautiful expression of love that I will one day experience with my husband.

Related Scriptures: "So God created man in his own image, in the image of God he created him; male and female he created them. God blessed them and said to them, 'Be fruitful and increase in number; fill the earth and subdue it'" (Genesis 1:27–28).

The entire book of Song of Songs (Solomon).

Ungodly Belief: If I act like nothing ever happened, the memories and emotions will eventually go away.

Godly Belief: I will speak out what is right, and I know God will be my refuge. I receive healing so that I no longer live in fear but can experience true peace.

Related Scriptures: "I will heal my people and will let them enjoy abundant peace and security" (Jeremiah 33:6).

"Have nothing to do with the fruitless deeds of darkness, but rather expose them" (Ephesians 5:11).

"My inmost being will rejoice when your lips speak what is right" (Proverbs 23:16).

"He whose walk is blameless is kept safe, but he whose ways are perverse will suddenly fall" (Proverbs 28:18).

INDEX TO PRAYERS

SOURCES

Alcorn, Nancy. *Keys to Walking in Freedom* CD series. Nashville: Mercy Ministries. (www.mercyministries.com).

Anderson, Neil T. *The Bondage Breaker*. Eugene, OR: Harvest House, 2006.

Anderson, Neil T. *Victory over the Darkness*. Ventura, CA: Regal, 2000. (www.ficm.org).

Capps, Charles. *God's Creative Power for Healing*. Tulsa: Harrison House, 1991. (www.charlescapps.com).

Kylstra, Chester, and Betsy Kylstra. *Restoring the Foundations*. Hendersonville, NC: Proclaiming His Word, Inc., 2001. (www.phw.org).

ABOUT MERCY MINISTRIES

*M*ercy Ministries exists to provide opportunities for young women to experience God's unconditional love, forgiveness, and life-transforming power. We provide residential programs free of charge to young women ages 13–28 who are dealing with life-controlling issues such as eating disorders, self-harm, addictions, sexual abuse, unplanned pregnancy, and depression. Our approach addresses the underlying roots of these issues by addressing the whole person—spiritual, physical, and emotional—and produces more than just changed behavior; the Mercy Ministries program changes hearts and stops destructive cycles.

Founded in 1983 by Nancy Alcorn, Mercy Ministries currently operates in three states and in Australia, Canada, New Zealand, and the UK, with plans for additional US and international locations underway. We are blessed to have connecting relationships with many different Christian congregations but are not affiliated with any church, organization, or denomination. Residents enter Mercy Ministries on a voluntary basis and stay an average of six months. Our program includes life-skills training and educational opportunities that help ensure the success of our graduates. Our goal is for each young woman to not only complete the program but also to discover the purpose for her life and bring value to her community as a productive citizen.

VIOLATED

For more information, visit our Web site at
www.mercyministries.com.

Mercy Ministries of America
www.mercyministries.com

Mercy Ministries Australia
www.mercyministries.com.au

Mercy Ministries Canada
www.mercycanada.com

Mercy Ministries UK
www.mercyministries.co.uk

Mercy Ministries New Zealand
www.mercyministries.org.nz

Mercy Ministries Peru

ABOUT THE AUTHOR

uring and after college, Nancy Alcorn, a native Tennessean, spent eight years working for the state of Tennessee at a correctional facility for juvenile delinquent girls and investigating child abuse cases. Working for the state allowed her to experience firsthand the secular programs, which were not producing permanent results exemplified by changed lives. Nancy saw many of the girls pass the age of eighteen and end up in the women's prison system because they never got the real help they needed. She knew lasting change would never come as the result of any government system.

After working for the state, she was appointed Director of Women for Nashville Teen Challenge, where she worked for two years. Through her experience, she came to realize that only Jesus could bring restoration into the lives of these girls who were deeply hurting and desperately searching for something to fill the void they felt in their hearts. She knew God was revealing a destiny that would result in her stepping out to do something to help young women.

In January 1983, determined to establish a program in which lives would truly be transformed, Nancy moved to Monroe, Louisiana, to start Mercy Ministries of America. God instructed Nancy to do three specific things to ensure His blessings on the ministry: (1) not to take any state or federal funding that might limit the freedom to teach Christian principles, (2) to accept girls free of charge, and (3) to always give at least 10 percent of all Mercy Ministries' donations to other Christian organizations and ministries. As Nancy has continued to be faithful to these three principles, God has been faithful to provide for every need of the ministry just as He promised.

In Monroe, Nancy began with a small facility for troubled girls. After adding on twice to make additional space in the original home, Nancy began to see the need for an additional home to meet the special needs of unwed mothers. For this dream to be realized on a debt-free basis, Nancy knew she would need to raise funds. No doubt, God knew the need and already had a plan in place.

One day, Nancy, exhausted from speaking at an evangelism conference in Las Vegas, boarded a plane for home. The man sitting next to her seemed ready for a chat. When he asked her how much money she had lost gambling, Nancy told him she hadn't gone to Vegas to gamble and shared briefly about Mercy Ministries with him. He seemed interested, so Nancy gave him a brochure as they parted. About four weeks later, this same man called Nancy to ask her for more details about Mercy Ministries and said he felt compelled to help in some way. It was then that Nancy told him about the plans for the unwed mothers' home. He told her he had been adopted when he was five days old. His heart was so touched that he wrote a check to Mercy Ministries for the exact amount needed to help build the second Mercy Ministries house debt-free.

You can read Nancy's entire story in her book *Echoes of Mercy.*